Wandering through Irish Legend, Lore and More

Time Travel through Ireland

David Lundberg

Zante

ZANTE

Zante Publishing
6304 Birkdale Court
Greensboro, North Carolina 27410
info@zantepub.com

ISBN 978-0-9763246-5-2

Also by David Lundberg

Olympic Wandering
Time Travel through Greece

Wandering with Fred and Dante
Time Travel through Italy

Acknowledgments

I am indebted to my wife, Vasso for her encouragement and fine help in editing this manuscript.

To my ancestors and relatives, the people of Ireland, past, present and future, I extend my respect and affection.

To Vasso

Island Lost in Time

Lost in time on northern seas,
A land of ice and snow,
Linked by a land-bridge,
To larger world below.

Warming earth brought rising seas,
Land-strip disappeared,
Ice and snow retreated,
Green forests then appeared.

Birds, animals, then men,
Followed close behind,
As their world brightened,
They sought what they could find.

First came huts of wood,
And then an age of stone,
Hard rock for temple-tombs,
To worship the great sun.

That sun was all-important,
A source of shining gold,
Giving life to their crops,
A mirror to their soul.

The seasons were a pattern,
The moon's month showed the same,
Days and nights the shortest span,
Part of God's great game?

Light lengthened each new day,
It reached a summer peak,
Then slowly it declined,
In winter solstice weak.

Magic forces did abound,
Of this, they were quite sure,
The mystery was great,
They hungered to know more.

Men with imagination,
Made tales 'round the fire,
Looking at that light at night,
Helped them to inspire.

Those stories fashioned spirits,
Explaining life's mysteries,
Small, good people, fairies,
Fables, myths and fantasies.

To Hibernia

I wake to sunshine on my back,
It flows on to the sea,
Shining 'cross the waves,
Coming home to me.

That yellow light moves behind,
And upward to my left,
Brightness fills my world,
And warmth embraces it.

Slow, the circle moves above,
Then falls into the sea,
Splashing out bright colors,
As far as eye can see.

My land is Iberia,
South and on the sea,
Earth is parched and barren,
Hardly ever free.

Darkness comes, I sink in sand,
I dream of other stars,
Above the water further west,
Far from heat and wars.

My friends build a sturdy ship,
Not fast, but very sound,
To travel on the ocean,
Hope is westward bound.

We launch out toward the sunset,
Our wind comes from the south,
It drives us to the north,
Very far, far out.

Birds flying high above us,
And heading back for home,
We sail on and on,
Now we're quite alone.

Our hearts are thrilled and fearful,
Through darkness, rolling seas,
We're chilled and wet on those dark nights,
Then warm on blinding days.

Birds now disappear, they're gone,
Blue seas, dark and swelling,
They push our craft on further yet,
Our journey seems unending.

Then birds return, now leading us,
To a world where no sun sets,
Cool and very still,
A place where one forgets.

Green rises from gray waters,
Those birds are much more bold,
Now they are one focus,
They have a single goal.

Sails come down from above,
The ship grinds on the sand,
Trees and many bushes,
Now are close at hand.

The men are proud, the women fair,
Small groups sing in the night,
They circle all around
a flickering firelight.

Drums and bows and flutes,
Eyes bright in every place,
Their brilliant smiles are lighting
Each and every face.

Cattle, crops and hunting
Are just for us alone,
Other tribes unspoken,
Kings for now unknown.

Sea and forest yield their meat,
Clouds spread their ample rain,
And in its proper time,
The land gives golden grain.

We build homes of wood and thatch,
We learn to hunt and fish,
And slowly, smiling women
Provide to us our wish.

We call this land Hibernia,
Iberia fades away,
Our children learn to laugh,
And then they grow and play.

Myths

Ireland has its heroes,
Likewise, heroines,
They walk the lanes of his-try,
While haunting old ruins.

First came the Druids,
In mists of the past,
Mysterious, little-known,
A high and priestly class.

They watched the flights of birds,
Beneath an ancient oak,
In this, they saw the future,
They gazed up through the smoke.

They memorized long poems,
As hard as iron bars,
Minds contained vast galaxies,
Words like endless stars.

An ancient stone dolmen,
Appeared as their altar,
What and how they worshiped,
Is lost to us thus far.

They gave the people meaning,
In this confusing world,
Source of strength and purpose,
They made their spirits bold.

And likewise came the poets,
Crafting words quite fine,
They also worked with rhythm,
Memorizing every line.

Those bards preserved the culture,
History had its place,
And in the souls of Irish,
Their past, unending race.

Bronze, Gold and Iron

Next came the Age of Bronze,
As mankind did go on,
Eire had much copper,
Mixed tin from far abroad.

Some bronze was for the battle,
And some for ornament,
Craftsmen fashioned both,
What mankind could invent.

Eire had precious gold,
Mines found quite a store,
Discs and torques made circles,
Like carved stones long before.

Finally came the iron,
With those fighting Celts,
Next great race to mix their blood,
Swords hanging from their belts.

Brought language and their fights,
Forts from which to strike,
Ringed ones on higher ground,
Some on islands in the lake.

Clans formed into tribes,
To seek the upper hand,
Stealing gold and cattle,
To gain the other's land.

Heroes, feasts and love affairs,
They often were war-worn,
Weapons, war and bravery,
More legends being born.

Rushing naked into battle,
With demonic scream,
Their enemies quite frightened,
Like in some horrid dream.

At times, their form did change,
Struck terror in others' hearts,
Shape-shift and warp-spasm,
Shooting fear like dreadful darts.

Celts soon owned the landscape,
Strength filled every soul,
And to this very day,
They make this Ireland whole.

Gods

Like the ancient Greeks,
Eire had many gods,
They mingled with the people,
Sometimes, quite at odds.

Gods and people close,
More alike than far apart,
The world did have a closeness,
Today, we've lost somewhat.

Those gods had special qualities,
Like all of us still do,
We could understand them,
So very long ago.

Now we are quite different,
God seems to have strayed,
Perhaps we are confused,
We've lost the ancient way.

In that old, old world,
Queens had a certain way,
Brigid, goddess of fertility,
Had a certain way to lay,

Babd was confusing,
Sometimes she was a crow,
Other times quite lovely,
As pure as driven snow.

Boann was another,
We hear of her still,
River Boyne sings her name,
Goddess of waters chill.

Daghdna was the king,
The gods were also odd,
His club was full of death,
His cauldron, full of food.

Oghma began the alphabet,
We see those fine marks still,
Upon the ancient stones,
On churches, tombs and hill.

Many other deities,
In our ancient minds,
Made trips to other worlds,
To find different kinds.

The Celts knew the stars,
And the planets, too,
Celebrate the seasons,
Festivals with much ado.

People, kings and gods,
That is our larger world,
It's good to remember,
We are not alone.

Legends

After gods came legends,
Great women, also men,
Strong and heroic,
Roaming mount and glen.

Queen Mebd was a terror,
As good as many men,
Not one king could best her,
In battle or in bed.

The Cattle Raid of Cooley,
This epic now is told,
Cows were good as money,
The best like precious gold.

Also there was Cuchulain,
Killed a hundred of Mebd's men,
Resting after battle,
Mebd's army took revenge.

Upon his a-rising,
Ready, war to wage,
A murderous warp-spasm,
Unleashed a fearsome rage.

His look, fierce and dreadful,
Hundreds more were slain,
Women, horses, warriors,
All dead upon the plain.

Mebd made peace with the hero,
But secretly she schemed,
At last she did succeed,
The great one finally slain.

The Finn

Then rose Finn MacCool,
Giant of Irish past,
Descended from the Druids,
Taught by them at last.

He built the Giant's Causeway,
A marvel to this day,
Six-sided stone columns,
They point out his way.

A bridge o'er to Scotland,
From northern Irish Sea,
Only gods could make those steps,
That's very plain to see.

Finn led the Fianna,
A rebel Irish clan,
They fiercely fought for freedom,
With any one at hand.

And that's the tale of Ireland,
Fighters, strong and free,
That is the legacy,
They pass to you and me.

They create a wondrous model,
Race of the long robe,
A humble, proud people,
Spread around the globe.

Good at procreation,
They've wandered far and wide,
Their blood flows through the veins,
Wherever men reside.

Patrick

I gaze across the water,
I sense that other land,
And though I do not see it,
I feel its strong demand.

My heart on fire within me,
I want to share that glow,
With those who once enslaved me,
I so want them to know.

They stole me from my father's land,
One dark and stormy night,
I walked upon our sandy shore,
Careless, out of parents' sight.

What the pirates did to me,
Seems a bitter plight,
They carried me 'cross the sea,
But God then made it right.

I tended sheep, cold hillsides,
Far from my mother's arms,
At first, it was quite bitter,
I came to know God's charms.

Sometimes what seems quite ugly,
Later becomes God's plan,
His ways unknown to men,
Seen by a single man.

Six years among the flocks,
I became a full-grown man,
A voice then called out to me,
Return to Briton land.

I walked down to the sea,
And went aboard a ship,
Sailing east and homeward,
Railing strong within my grip.

We landed on my island,
We started north to home,
Days and nights meant nothing,
My heart was not alone.

Parents did not believe me,
They thought it was a lie,
My mother looked into my eyes,
Fell to her knees and cried.

Life began again for them,
But not, of course, for free,
Fire burned within my heart,
Always drawing me.

My friends and I departed,
Trained in a holy place,
We asked return to Ireland,
Strange and pagan place.

We landed on my captive land,
The people were the same,
Fierce and red and violent,
Only I had changed.

I told them gods they knew,
Were everywhere the same,
Under one umbrella,
And Christ-ian was his name.

Shamrock showed the three-in-one,
A simple cross could stand,
Fire in one's heart,
Proof of God's great plan.

That is the faith I brought them,
The best that I could be,
It seemed so very little,
To what hillsides gave to me.

The C Men

Christians attracted C men,
Strange that this should be,
Local Irish monks,
Often named with magic C.

Columcille came early,
From Conaill family,
A monastery maker,
Warrior-monk was he.

Columbanus was another,
An Irish émigré,
Built monasteries in Europe,
From France to Italy.

Ciaran was from Connacht,
Built great Clonmacnoise,
In center of this Ireland,
Fine, strategic choice.

Where the river Shannon,
Intersects the east-west road,
Like a mighty cross,
Centered on this great abode.

Wheels of time now spinning,
Europe turning dark,
Who could guess small Ireland,
Would keep alive the spark.

That fire of great learning,
Was left to Irish scribes,
They copied books of wisdom,
Letters bright and quite alive.

Writing became an art-form,
Still preserved today,
Treasures like the Book of Kells,
Still point us to the Way.

Ostmen

Longboats came from the east,
Wide and very fast,
The crews had not captains,
Long oars, a single mast.

The men were nearly giants,
Long hair down past their arms,
Heavy swords and axes,
Searching for new farms.

Took all that they wanted,
Food and gold and slaves,
Many often plundered,
Others simply stayed.

Irish fought each other,
Plus new men from the east,
Stealing cows and sheep,
Never any rest.

Eastmen took local wives,
Settled after all,
After a few years,
Children grew quite tall.

They lived near the waters,
Some became new lords,
Clustered in their groups,
Towns named for new fiords.

Taking on the Irish culture,
And Saint Patrick's God,
Speaking now in Gaelic,
Their roots sunk deep in sod.

Blended with the Eire-men,
You can see them still,
Heads held high and skyward,
Walking where they will.

Brian Boru

Fighting, fighting, fighting,
Is that all the Irish do?
Obviously not,
They've lots of children, too.

Many kings a-warring,
No one at the top,
Alliances always crumbled,
Didn't make them stop.

A warrior rose in the south,
He had some family aid,
Father, brother before him,
Showed him how to raid.

He outdid them both,
Became the high king,
It didn't last so long,
Ended with him dying.

Songs written about him,
This Brian Boru,
Made him a mythic figure,
A great warrior, too.

He spawned another clan,
O'Brien is its name,
Did not stop the fighting,
Ireland, just the same.

Land of tribes always,
Another name for clan,
This built a deep closeness,
For family and the land.

Normans

Next came the English-Normans,
At first from northern France,
Just simple sell-swords,
They joined the Irish dance.

And like so many others,
Seduced by Ireland's charms,
Liking what they saw then,
Laid down their violent arms.

More Irish than the Irish,
Soon was said of them,
As their Viking cousins,
They blended right on in.

Soon England seemed quite distant,
At least in Norman hearts,
Distracted by other struggles,
The English turned their backs.

When they were awakened,
Saw Eire might slip away,
They sent Protestant bosses,
Keep Ireland in their sway.

This sent, of course, a friction,
That's never gone away,
Politics of religion,
Continue to this day.

The churches not much different,
Nor the DNA,
But power and money,
E'er seem to lead the way.

Cities Unimportant

Irish are country people,
In their very soul,
Never had large cities,
Didn't need that role.

Outside of modern Dublin,
People spread more evenly,
Like dear Kilkenny,
Twenty thousand souls, ... a city?

Even other places,
Belfast, Cork, Galway,
Are really just large towns,
Meeting friends along the way.

Perhaps that is the lesson,
Even for big-town folk,
Cities can crush the spirit,
People do not count.

Yet, even in large Dublin,
In pubs with music free,
We are friends and family,
Any one can see.

Again, it's those we love,
Who pierce the Irish heart,
Eire, still a bunch of clans,
They make that love an art.

Singing and joking,
Pints lifted in the air,
They have the gift of gab,
And kindness, that is clear.

Monasteries

Monasteries became the rage,
Scattered all about,
Led by some strong monk,
With heart quite firm and stout.

Others clustered 'round him,
They followed leadership,
Irish in tune with Spirit,
With men who have a grip.

Stone centers rose from nothing,
Religious labor cheap,
Working hard for their God,
Sure of their giant leap.

They raised ample grain,
'round cloisters with large fields,
Turning it to food and spirits,
Beer, bread, all proper yields.

So those places prospered,
Grew rich and quite free,
Far from hand of Rome,
And the pa-tri-archy.

So then, rose strong women,
Like an Irish prophecy,
Deidre, and then Brigid,
Following Mehb's legacy.

We see it still in Ireland,
Where women rose and shone,
The pirate queen O'Malley,
McAleese and Robinson.

This will long continue,
The template has been set,
We thank God for Irish mothers,
Myself, and countless yet.

Cromwell

The English found one Cromwell,
Skilled and quite ruth-less,
He came in mighty force,
Where his army went, laid waste.

Ireland fell to its knees,
Oliver did his job,
But, England soon grew tired,
Of Cromwell and his blood.

A short return of Catholics,
Came to the English isle,
It did not last so long,
Very brief, short while.

Then came back the Protestants,
They firmly were in sway,
Warring ceased in Ireland,
Oppression was the way.

Politics long lasting,
More than two hundred years,
Again the fight for freedom,
Marked by blood and tears.

Ireland never quite united,
Too many warring kings,
Perhaps now that is why,
They're good in boxing rings.

Skilled and smart indeed they are,
As always they have been,
Perhaps that's why they always rise,
Time and time, again.

Fighters, writers, engineers,
Adept with sword and pen,
Musicians, dancers, singers,
Skills spring, now and then.

Friendly, warm, free-standing,
Lusty women, headstrong men,
Throw off shackles, one by one,
Freedom, ... only question, ... when?

Protestants Ascendant

Protestants ascendant,
Has marked modern times,
Confusing see-saw battles,
Many, many crimes.

It's hard to see a standard,
In this tug-of-war,
Neither English nor Irish,
Have fixed it all, thus far.

If there is a constant,
In this struggle o'er the years,
It's been broken promises,
So, trust seldom appears.

When that faith does glimmer,
Appears between the sides,
The truly brave grasp at it,
In hope for better times.

It always seems quite shaky,
'tween groups who seem alike,
They claim they're both ethical,
Religions make them right.

Perhaps these new beliefs,
Have brought us far away,
From the spirit God once gave us,
Maybe we've lost our way.

I'm just one person writing,
What do I truly know?
Many cocksure prophets,
Just like long ago.

Perhaps things don't change much,
That is my honest guess,
We ne'er advance a lot,
Human nature does not progress.

I'd like to think differently,
Would be comforting to know,
Our world could advance,
Nobler, better, ... so.

The Shift

First were Irish Protestants,
Grattan, Tone, Parnell,
Then came the Catholics,
Collins, Eamon, O'Connell.

In the 1700s,
A subtle shift began,
Those Irish Protestants,
Thought of their whole land.

A man named Henry Grattan,
Rose in Parliament,
He pushed for Irish free trade,
Amazing, it was sent.

Grattan then argued,
For Irish independent,
This was also granted,
With huge restrictions yet.

Next came Mr. Wolfe Tone,
Another Protestant,
He reached out to Catholics,
England turned resistant.

Wolfe Tone pushed harder,
England came down hard,
Tone died in prison,
Battle-lines were drawn.

Then arose a Catholic,
One Daniel O'Connell,
Born in County Kerry,
Business family as well.

Trained to be a lawyer,
Had an Irish, silver tongue,
No judge could stand up to him,
His words always stung.

In a daring move,
The Catholic ran for Parliament,
He won and forced the English hand,
To London he was sent.

He pushed for Ireland's freedom,
That was his clear intent,
Later, mayor of Dublin,
On and on he went.

Daniel was a fighter,
But had Achilles' heel,
He would not do violence,
Brits thwarted his strong zeal.

His great monster meetings,
Held to make Eire free,
Were finally folded,
Daniel wanted no melee.

But, he pushed that cause of freedom,
A giant step along the way,
Dan played his part,
Liberty, another day.

The Famine

No ode to Ireland,
Could ever be complete,
Without talk of famine,
Which dropped her to her feet.

There never was a crop,
So suited to a land,
As that potato was,
Tailor-made for Ireland.

Brought from Amer-ica,
It grew like a weed,
Highly nutritious,
Met all the families' need.

On just a few acres,
Each family could survive,
Raising crops and children,
Both did strongly thrive.

Then came sudden sickness,
One season saw fields fail,
On for several more,
Eire went very pale.

Massive starvation,
Drove an exodus,
Skeletons sailing,
Away in coffin ships.

Those who did make it,
'cross those angry seas,
Struggling for new lives,
Without that plant disease.

Worked at what they could,
In lands where they did fly,
Building mighty cities,
That pointed to the sky.

Those stubborn folks from Eire,
Planted their hardy seed,
Now their genes have spread,
Wherever they did breed.

They headed to the setting sun,
As far as they could go,
America and Canada,
The vast Pacific road.

Building railroads, bridges, tunnels,
Running many bars,
Joining the police force,
Reaching for the stars.

Wit and Wisdom

Irish wit and wisdom,
Flow down the centuries,
Ready with a playful joke,
Everyone agrees.

Very quick to laugh,
'course they love to spar,
Tongue and many words,
That's the verbal war.

Wisdom is more earthy,
So honed through many years,
It comes from endless times,
With struggles and with tears.

Both are long abiding,
Part of the Irish dance,
Like a giant see-saw,
Strike a fine balance.

Life is not all serious
Nor is it just for play,
Perhaps both are needed,
For us to make our way.

Life still continues,
Every single day,
Ancient ways show a path,
For our earthly stay.

Maybe preparation,
For some distant goal,
As nature long continues,
Rolling on for all.

The Writers

Multitudes of writers,
From all ends of the isle,
Heaney, Yeats, and Swift,
Joyce, Beckett, and Wilde.

Many, many others,
Too numerous to name,
Used pen to scratch their thoughts,
Minds that were not tame.

At that turn of century,
Arose a man named Joyce,
Dubliner by birth,
And in his heart by choice.

A rebel from beginning,
And brilliant just as well,
Excelling in his schools,
As later times would tell.

Took diploma from new UCD,
Then on to Paris, France,
Medicine did not suit him,
He did not there advance.

Back and forth, agitated,
Ireland for a while,
Met Nora, was smitten,
Restless, again exile.

To Zurich as a teacher,
Then to Tri-es-te,
He managed to find contacts,
All along the way.

Finally back to Paris,
He lived for quite a while,
Did a lot of writing,
Eyes became fragile.

He still continued writing,
On and on, his art,
Zurich saw his end,
Dublin, in his heart.

Yeats

Another one was Yeats,
A complicated man,
Brilliant mystic in beginning,
For sure he had no plan.

His life was tormented,
By unrequited love,
Proposed to Maud five times,
She would not approve.

His poetry was brilliant,
Won a Nobel Prize,
He loved those Irish myths,
Spirits, dreams, fantasize.

Like that Mister Joyce,
Of restless Irish race,
Yeats died in southern France,
Moving place to place.

His bones returned to Sligo,
Where his heart was fond,
That wild west greenery,
Spirits he dreamed upon.

Beckett

Then came Samuel Beckett,
His family somewhat rich,
After education,
He got the traveling itch.

Off he went to Paris,
Made friends with Mister Joyce,
Opposites in writing,
Each with his own voice.
Joyce was always adding,
To everything he wrote,
While Beckett was subtracting,
Minimalist of note.

Collins and Eamon

Collins and Eamon,
At first, they were allied,
Turn of century,
Seemed a proper time.

One a man of action,
The other, more diplomat,
That ancient Irish theme,
Couldn't get along enough.

Collins struck the deal,
Best that he could do,
Eamon would not go along,
Familiar Irish stew.

Then came civil war,
Happens now and then,
Brother against brother,
Even with the best of men.

Michael was slain,
Not a big surprise,
Passion often stronger,
Than a compromise.

That man, de Valera,
Led Ireland many years,
Brought her to the modern world,
Through heartache and through tears.

Eire rose to world-stage,
Free in her heart,
Stayed alone, independent,
Not a simple part.

The country has advanced,
It's been no easy load,
Ups and downs are countless,
Not a level road.

The Road to Freedom

Now that road to freedom,
Littered with names of men,
Taking different paths,
Always, now and then.

From north and south they rose,
If not with pen or speech,
Songs or guns they carried,
Whatever suited each.

That cry of liberty,
Swelled like a mighty sea,
Dashing 'gainst the rocks,
Of long-term tyranny.

The swell has not subsided,
Less angry, well perhaps,
But just as resolute,
Freedom never naps.

60

There always seem new battles,
Perhaps not so strange,
Always some oppression,
Whether church or state.

Now the fight more female,
Women, always resolute,
Hands on hips defiant,
'til freedom takes real root.

Is the fight now over?
No, ... here's the hardest part,
There's always some new ruler,
Who wants another's heart.

Boom

After the dust settled,
And Ireland was free,
The garden isle bloomed brighter,
For everyone to see.

Fish and meat and crops,
Continued very strong,
Bright minds were educated,
And, before too long,

Factories and banking,
Along with fine high-tech,
Propelled the Irish higher,
Racing neck to neck,

The Tiger did catch up,
With that great first-world.
Heading for sharp climax,
Then fell upon her sword.

It's a familiar story,
Often seen before,
Boom and bust for Eire,
Brought her to the floor.

Boxers who've been staggered,
Often rise again.
This is true of Ireland.
Persistence oft' can win.

Perhaps next time more cautious,
However, maybe not,
Human nature doesn't change,
Memory soon forgot.

Rising from the canvas,
Of the boxing ring of life,
Great fighters always carry on,
Through this world of strife.

Pubs

Today that ancient Ireland,
Still shines in modern eyes,
In countless pubs extended,
We see each clan's ties.

Gathering in old circles,
Like centuries before,
Friends come to sing and play,
Sharing sweet hu-mor.

There's very little envy,
That's the magic trick,
Kindness reaches outward,
Friendship is such a kick.

They welcome each one's efforts,
At strumming or with song,
Or listen to long stories,
Told with rhythmic tone.

Smiles seem ever present,
With those melodies,
Happiness imbibed,
Along with countless ales

The publicans do prosper,
From Irish ca-marad-erie,
Pints just keep on coming,
They accompany the glee.

'til the night grows older,
Eyelids begin to droop,
Folks begin to shuffle home,
Fun will finally stop.

At least 'til next evening,
It starts up once again,
Songs and stories on and on,
Never seems to end.

Guinness

In great Dublin city,
The very best view,
Of the city skyline,
Is where we lift a brew.

At the Guinness warehouse,
On the topmost floor,
Is a glassed-in bar,
See almost to the moor.

Arthur Guinness started it,
His vision gazed quite far,
Irish liked dark porter,
He crafted like a star.

Used water from Wicklow,
Mountains to the south,
Nutritious, roasted barley,
Tart taste within your mouth.

Guinness was a kind one,
Plus great business-man,
His employees seldom suffered,
Their families did not want.

'though he was Church of Ireland,
He restored Saint Patrick's hall,
Great Catholic cathedral,
Art was Irish, after all.

Arthur's gone two hundred years,
The brewery still remains,
The beating heart of Dublin,
Kindness there still reigns.

Smithwicks

Another beer is Smith-icks,
This one a tasty ale,
Family started in Kilkenny,
Now that's a charming tale.

Built on monastery ground,
Where monks made that ale,
Much to the brothers' pleasure,
Drink never did go stale.

I visited the brewery,
During Kilkenny stay,
Our tour-guide drew the samples,
In a reverential way.

As red as Irish hair tops,
Is this creamy drink,
Somehow seems quite fitting.
Tends to make you think.

Strands of Irish culture
Like a sunny braid,
Passed down those centuries,
As Ireland was made.

The job is never finished,
With each new crop of kids,
The garden isle rolls along,
Flame-hair still lifts eyelids.

Medieval streets, they beckon,
Castles, churches, they remain,
The stones feel ghosts passing,
Down each ancient lane.

River Liffey

The good Liffey River,
Splits Dublin west to east,
That city hugs the Irish Sea,
Liffey flows into the coast.

Almost a dozen bridges,
Cross this fine divide,
North Dublin on one bank,
The South, the other side.

Pathways are quite varied,
Just like Irish folk,
Some bridges very modern,
Others just to walk.

The people-bridge Ha' Penny,
Was built so long ago,
To replace the ferries,
That shuttled to and fro.

Half-penny was the toll,
To walk above the waves,
Guess cost was reasonable,
They strolled across in droves.

More bridges, they came later,
Some just concrete roads,
Others, new suspension ones,
Art-forms to carry loads.

Today, in bustling Dublin,
Bridges often jammed,
Buses, cars and people cross,
Where those boats once steamed.

Wexford

Traveling down to Wexford,
Along the Irish Sea,
Passing pretty coastal towns,
Prosperous, they must be.

Founded by the Vikings,
Such was Wexford town,
As the name implies,
New fiord for Norse to own.

Once a mighty port,
But nature made a dent,
Harbor silted up,
To Rosslare shipping went.

Still a lovely city,
Lively pubs and such,
A city for the Irish,
Beyond the tourist crush.

"Sunny Southeast" they call it,
That has to bring a smile,
Means they have a few less clouds,
Than rest of Emerald Isle.

Lovely walking town,
Has a rocky past,
Those cobblestone streets,
Blood and battles, alas.

Today, migrant birds,
Rest upon her shores,
Wildlife is abundant,
Find food in shallow stores.

Kilkenny

Many Kils in Ireland,
The dearest one to me,
Is the only city,
Distant from the sea.

Kilkenny, the medieval,
Fascin-ating history,
Retains the nostalgia,
Like any great story.

Yes, she has a river,
So many towns here do,
Straddling the waters,
Pleasant place to go.

Tis' the place of hurling,
Ancient Irish sport,
Like a hockey stick,
That never touches dirt.

Has an awesome castle,
And fine churches, too,
Stories of the witches,
Many years ago.

Here, I love the pubs,
Singing, oh, so vast,
But, also great orators,
Who carry Irish past.

They are a time machine,
That rumbles on today,
Perhaps the best message,
To guide us on our way.

Killarney

Heading west in Ireland,
Hard to miss this town,
Set in scenic country,
Lakes, mountains of renown.

Another Kil, it's Larney,
Victim of success,
Much to see around it,
Business a tad excess.

Mountain lakes pristine,
Views are very grand,
Tourist buses constant,
Still a magic land.

The fabled Ring of Kerry,
Is a lovely treat,
Birthplace of O'Connell,
Patriot, hard to beat.

Much to see and do,
Busy place for sure,
Fun-seekers look for leisure,
Always something more.

South of Valentia Island,
The famous Skellig isles,
Once held monasteries,
No more for those exiles.

Now the birds and tourists,
Enjoy those craggy rocks,
Rising from the seas,
As seen from ferry docks.

Dingle

All the way to Dingle,
Far west and on the sea,
Small fishing port, now tourists,
They've found variety.

It still retains its flavor,
Despite the visi-tors,
Culture is not vanished,
Though crowded with new bars.

Far southwest of Ireland,
Has stunning sights galore,
Rock houses, magic vistas,
The stuff of Irish lore.

Ancient mountains, sailors,
They traveled further west,
Saint Brendan, navigator,
Preceded all the rest.

It's said he reached America,
But, who can truly say,
So many legends written,
Just memories today.

Today, that Dingle harbor,
Has dolphin for mascot,
It plays with tourist boats,
Perhaps it's not forgot.

Over many centuries,
That bond with sea is clear,
Mermaids, seals and humans,
All God's creatures dear.

Up the Coast

Up the western coast,
Great part of Ireland,
Scenery alluring,
Here along land's end.

Heart of Irish music,
Instruments galore,
Dedicated artists,
Keep on playing more.

Past the Cliffs of Moher,
Windswept Doolin, special place,
Lanes lined with cows, pastures,
Village of a special face.

There's country in this town,
Still reverence for the land,
Aran Isles in the distance,
Songs are close at hand,

County Clare, the heartbeat,
Precision tunes abound,
In many nook and cranny,
Sessions can be found.

Music town of Ennis,
Pubs line the main street,
Players concentrated,
Every beat complete.

We look on to Galway,
Westport and beyond,
Stretching north to Donegal,
Easy to grow fond.

Galway

Halfway up that coast,
With the greatest bay,
Lies a town of festivals,
Artsy, alive Gal-way.

City of much granite,
Solid building blocks,
Carved from local quarries,
The place is built of rocks.

Behind hard-faced buildings,
Is a vibrant scene,
Music, happy people,
Constantly convene.

Center of Irish language,
That is this city,
Across the river Corrib,
Sits fine uni-ver-sity.

Place of tribes and merchants,
That is its history,
Now a place of varied tastes,
Cheerful place to be.

Full of street musicians,
Some from different lands,
Adds to the spice of life,
Not just those Irish bands.

Jazz and jugglers, dancers,
All seem to have a go,
Of course, that Irish trad,
Is always there to glow.

Donegal

Donegal, the rustic,
Perched at world's end,
Unending, lovely vistas,
Forever they extend.

Fishing ports and mountains,
Gardens, they compete,
Cast a magic spell,
Nature seems complete.

It does have good-sized places,
Letterkenny is not small,
Donegal town is cozy,
It's simple after all.

Poets, ghosts, and banshees,
Remain with us a while,
This county seems quite mystic,
Like much of Emerald Isle,

More land than it has people,
Homes spread far apart,
For those from crowded cities,
Strikes loneliness in heart.

Yet nature is enduring,
Much more than any man,
We simply pass the torch of life,
To next one in our clan.

We're just passing through,
Life, we know endures,
Perhaps the earth is greater,
Than all our human chores.

Ode

I've tried to speak of Ireland,
Of what I've grown to know,
Ancient land of people,
I came to see their show.

Spirit springs from the earth,
It's like a mighty shout,
Because of this, there's kinship,
Of this, there is no doubt.

The climate, land and green'ry,
Gives them a special soul,
Endures through generations,
And, so they have a role.

There's a special kindness,
Ready wit and banter quick,
Pride, humility, at once,
A very charming trick.

Independent spirits,
Forged so long ago,
Laughing, lyric minds,
Songs and stories grow.

Sharp brains made great writing,
There won't be a demise,
Unless the earth stops spinning,
Or the sun forgets to rise.

Nature makes different people,
All around this world,
Thank God, She made the Irish,
Hearts of such fine gold.

About the Author

David Cassidy Lundberg has been a warehouse supervisor, an environmental engineer, and a university professor.

Dr. Lundberg has lived in various places in North America and in several European countries. For many years, he spent part of his summers in Greece. Now, he and his wife, Vasso, spend their summers in Ireland and their winters in North Carolina.

Made in United States
Orlando, FL
02 December 2021

10960612R00052